RUDOLF STEINER (1861–1925) called his spiritual philosophy 'anthroposophy', meaning 'wisdom of the human being'. As a highly developed seer, he based his work on direct knowledge and perception of spiritual dimensions. He initiated a modern and universal 'science of spirit', accessible to anyone willing to exercise clear and unprejudiced thinking.

From his spiritual investigations Steiner provided suggestions for the renewal of many activities, including education (both general and special), agriculture, medicine, economics, architecture, science, philosophy, religion and the arts. Today there are thousands of schools, clinics, farms and other organizations involved in practical work based on his principles. His many published works feature his research into the spiritual nature of the human being, the evolution of the world and humanity, and methods of personal development. Steiner wrote some 30 books and delivered over 6000 lectures across Europe. In 1924 he founded the General Anthroposophical Society, which today has branches throughout the world.

PEARLS OF THOUGHT
WORDS OF WISDOM

A selection of quotations by
RUDOLF STEINER

Compiled and introduced by Daniel Baumgartner

RUDOLF STEINER PRESS

Translated by Matthew Barton

Rudolf Steiner Press,
Hillside House, The Square
Forest Row, RH18 5ES

E-mail: office@rudolfsteinerpress.com

www.rudolfsteinerpress.com

Published by Rudolf Steiner Press 2015

Originally published in German under the title *Perlen des Denkens* by Rudolf Steiner Verlag, Basel, in 2008

A catalogue record for this book is available from the British Library

Print book ISBN: 978 1 85584 413 1
Ebook ISBN: 978 1 85584 454 4

Cover by Morgan Creative
Typeset by DP Photosetting, Neath, West Glamorgan
Printed and bound in Great Britain by 4edge Limited, Essex

Contents

Only rarely does someone wholly express their full individuality in a book.

About this Book

Like pearls in the oyster, pearls of wisdom lie hidden in texts and are easily overlooked. They keep their light under a bushel, serving a framework and context of thought. If we draw them out they begin to shine, revealing their translucent facets and intrinsic harmony. These small, self-sufficient verbal universes are real finds. In contrast to the prevailing view that meaning arises only in context, they show us that the opposite can also be true: they acquire enhanced meaning in isolation, mysteriously turning out to be independent of thoughts and phrases that precede or follow them. In the collective of sentences they stand out as individuals: like prime numbers in the arithmetic of thinking, or tasty morsels of philosophical insight.

The pearls of thought selected here bear witness to Rudolf Steiner's style of speech and thinking. Unlike his contemporary Nietzsche, he did not hammer his readers but used a far finer implement. Whereas Nietzsche bangs nails in with forceful articulation, Rudolf Steiner continually seeks to mould and sculpt his medium of language so that the idea feels at home in the form of language it inhabits. This is also why he dispenses with dramatic formulations, pointed emphasis or smugness. Instead of resorting to spectacular statement, he couches speculation — wholly in conformity with German idealism — in terms that wrestle gently with the dynamic energy and dignity of the world of ideas. Where Nietzsche strikes sparks and splinters from his anvil, Rudolf Steiner creates the conditions in which pearls of thought can cohere and coalesce. They often appear as the culmination of a sequence of thoughts, either in a whole sentence or else simply cast down as random phrase, as if waiting to be discovered and appreciated.

It is possible to gather up these pearls and thread them together to create new textures and striking panoramas that emerge from the interplay of transformed contexts. Thus dynamic constellations of thought arise, allowing us unusual and surprising access to Rudolf Steiner's philosophical thinking.

We should not expect smart aphorisms or complacent *bon mots* from this collection. The phrases are often very quiet if incontrovertible, while others may be mysterious or lead in strange, surprising directions. I have included phrases that have some relationship, whether centrally or peripherally, with philosophical issues, leaving out those containing anthroposophical terminology which require further explanation or definition. All the statements here, including the chapter headings, are to be found in Rudolf Steiner's written works. Apart from the opening motto overleaf, I did not draw on Steiner's spoken lectures.

Daniel Baumgartner

Truth is simple only for those
who first wrestle their way though multiplicity.
It is like a thread of many pearls.

1. Before anything else can be grasped, thinking itself must be

It cannot be denied: before anything else can be grasped, thinking itself must be.

Pure thinking, you see, is itself already a super-sensible activity.

Thinking alone can determine whether thinking is correct.

Thinking is the last link in the sequence of processes that create nature.

Our consciousness is not — as many people believe — the capacity to engender and preserve thoughts (ideas), but rather to perceive them.

Everything is ultimately resolved into thinking, and finds its place within it.

In thinking we have a principle that exists in and through itself.

Observation and thinking are the two points of departure for all human enquiry in so far as this is conscious.

Thinking exists *beyond* subject and object.

Living thinking is an intrinsic reality.

We can introduce a stronger impetus of will into ordinary conscious thinking than is present in it in our ordinary experience of the physical world.

Something that thinking could not encompass would be absurd.

If I think mathematically I am thinking about the sensory world but do not, at the same time, think *within* it.

In observing thinking we penetrate the fabric of the world.

There is nothing in the world that we know better than our thoughts.

Within the sensory world, realities continually correct our thinking.

The vocation of thinking is to solve the riddles that perception presents us with.

Especially when we consider its form as individual activity within our consciousness, our thinking is beholding—that is, it directs the gaze outwards towards what faces or confronts us.

The way a person thinks is the way he is.

Thought has proven itself the educator of the soul.

Thinking may play a secondary role in the emergence of world phenomena, but assuredly has a chief role in forming a view about them.

One may carry all the world's knowledge around in one's head, but genius never manifests without having a new thought.

Thinking has to strengthen itself to act with the vitality otherwise only present in sense perception; and thinking not reliant on memories must arise without sensory perception, instead experiencing its content in immediate presence, as one otherwise only finds in perception.

The distinctive nature of thinking is that the person thinking forgets thinking while he engages in it.

Ordinary thinking gives pictures of things and creatures; but this has as little reality as a mirror image has of the reflected object.

I can never observe my thinking in the present; instead, I can only use my thinking to reflect on the experiences I have had of my thinking process.

The whole human body is formed in such a way that its crowning glory is the brain, the organ of spirit.

Unprejudiced observation shows that nothing can be included as part of thinking that is not itself discovered *within* thinking.

However, there are people who wish to take 'inward' flight in order to evade the clarity of concepts.

I should never say that my individual subjectivity thinks, but rather that it lives by the grace of thinking.

All thinking leads only to the point where our experience of inner life must begin.

It is on this that our dual nature is based as human beings: we think and thus encompass ourselves and the rest of the world; but by means of thinking we must at the same time determine ourselves as an individual who confronts and is separate from things.

Someone who relies on his thinking knows that the surging tumult of events, the stormy chaos, will not destroy his tranquillity. He knows that all these tempests cannot unsettle him, because he understands them.

Our thinking is the interpreter who explains the gestures of experience.

Having driven thinking into inner life, we know from soul experience what it means to experience the transition from 'I think' to 'It thinks in me'.

In thinking we have the element that brings our specific individuality into union with the cosmos.

The human body is formed and constituted in a way that corresponds with thinking.

In sensing and feeling (and also perceiving) we are separate; in thinking we become the universal being which everything permeates.

The act of cognition is the synthesis of perception and concept.

Thinking is a human organ destined to observe things higher than the senses offer.

In ordinary consciousness we do not experience thinking, but through it, instead, we experience whatever is thought.

The full reality of a thing arises for us at the moment of observing it through the merging of concept and perception.

We can only grasp the nature of thinking through intuition.

The reality active in thinking is obliged to do two things: firstly, it suppresses the autonomous activity of the human organism, and secondly it replaces it.

The same substances and forces present also in the mineral kingdom are configured in the human body in such a way as to enable thinking to manifest.

Where the realm of freedom (in thinking and

action) begins, the individual ceases to be determined by laws of the genus.

What, in the rest of experience, must be drawn from somewhere else, if at all applicable to it — *the context of laws* — is already present in thinking at the first moment it manifests.

Thinking destroys the appearance implicit in perceiving and integrates our individual existence into the life of the cosmos.

Much is gained if we can realize that words are like *gestures*, able only to indicate the object they refer to, and that their actual content has nothing to do with the thought itself.

In observing thinking we live directly in a spiritual and self-sustaining weft of being.

The content of ideas in another person is also mine, and I will only continue to regard him as another while I perceive him; but no longer will do so as soon as I am thinking.

A philosopher is not someone who merely knows the sum of existing philosophical doctrines, or may also perhaps have added a few to them; but instead someone who has battled his way through with difficulty to the point not only of learning or conceiving realities, but experiencing them.

Since in thinking we experience a real lawfulness, a set of determining ideas, so the lawfulness of the rest of the world—which we do not experience—must also already lie contained within thinking.

Only when the world of ideas lights up out of our inner life and, in observing the world, we can see idea and sensory observation as a unified experience of cognition, do we have true reality before us.

Our human reason and intellect are as little accustomed to seeing the *sources* of truth in the world's whole existence as the eye can directly gaze upon the sun.

2. The world's content of ideas is founded on itself

The world's content of ideas is founded on itself, and intrinsically perfect.

In every single human individuality occurs the process that unfolds in the whole of nature: the creation of reality out of the idea.

There is only *one* thought content of the world.

The ideas of things are the content of what acts and creates within them.

The ground of the world has poured itself entirely into the world; it has not drawn back from the world in order to direct it from without but drives it from within; it has not withheld itself from the world.

The spirit is our eternal nourishment.

Our world of thoughts is thus an entity entirely

founded on itself, an inwardly self-contained, intrinsically perfect and perfected whole.

If we live truly in the world of ideas, we feel the being of the world working within us in incomparable warmth.

Thinking is an intrinsic totality, sufficient to itself; it may not exceed its own bounds without entering the void.

There is nothing further removed from mystical vagueness than the crystal-clear world of ideas, whose finest ramifications are sharply contoured.

One of the highest insights of the human spirit is the need to measure each thing by its own scale, and never to draw on experiences proper to another domain.

The way in which a thought content approaches us is a pledge that we here have reality before us.

Manifold consciousnesses think one and the same thing, merely approaching the whole truth from different angles.

However confused my thinking, in my actions daily

life urges upon me the laws that correspond to reality.

If we have the capacity for this, we see that the idea contains all that constitutes it, and that it presents us with all that can be asked of it.

What the spirit finds as unity in manifold reality it must find in the particularity of its immediate existence.

What can least be learned and thought but must instead be experienced is the principle that every thing must be observed in accordance with the innate individuality indwelling it.

For human beings to be their own lawgivers, they must relinquish all idea that the world is governed by powers that determine them from without.

The world's cultural content is not enriched by adding phenomena from elsewhere to the old stock, but rather by leading what eternally evolves to a new stage of development.

The active principle in all other things manifests in us as idea; the active principle in the human being is the idea that we ourselves produce.

A true individual will be the one whose feelings reach up furthest into the region of the ideal.

In grasping truth the soul unites with something that bears its own worth within it.

The human spirit never, in truth, goes beyond the bounds of reality in which we live; and it has no need to either, since the world contains everything necessary to explain it.

Only when the world of ideas lights up from soul life, and in looking upon the world we can place idea and sensory observation before our mind as unified cognitive experience, do we have true reality before us.

3. We do not act because we should but because we have the will to

Will without idea would be *nothing*.

The motive for action does not lie outside but within us.

To illumine the laws of our actions by the light of self-observation means to overcome the compulsion of motives.

The heart follows the head as long as the latter can find a particular direction.

If all natural processes are only manifestations of the idea, then human action is the active idea itself.

To perform an action for its own sake means to act from *love*.

The same power that rescues us in mid-life from becoming one with our bodily organism is also the creator of our free will.

We only act in real freedom when guided by love for an action, by devotion to objectivity.

And even if different people have different amounts of reason, it is identical in content. Where a person truly pledges himself to it rather than to subjective caprice and egotism, the will of one person cannot exclude that of the other but instead, in encountering it, will augment and support it.

The human being is his own lawgiver and does not allow laws to be dictated to him by some external power.

Our usual thinking capacity is extinguished when we observe our own will.

The path to the heart passes through the head.

By devoting ourselves to *living* thinking, we find both feeling and will, also in the depths of their reality. By turning away from thinking instead to 'sheer' feeling and will, we lose their true reality.

My action is free, its effect absolutely lawful.

Love is the motive for action.

In will, the soul knows itself to be surrendered to a spiritual activity that integrates us into a super-sensible context of reality, from which we only sunder ourselves through the subjective will of ordinary consciousness.

Will is sovereign.

Love for our work — not for its success — is the only thing that advances us.

In science the *idea* must be our guiding star, and in action *love* must be.

Every insight you seek only in order to enrich your knowledge, only to accumulate inner treasures, leads you away from your path; but every insight that you seek in order to grow more mature in the quest for human enhancement and the evolution of the world takes you a step forward.

The capacity for love is grounded in the human organization.

Inevitably, from time to time, there will appear radical destroyers of cultural achievements, minds who wish to rebuild everything from the founda-tions up.

I am not directly guided by what is commonly accepted, general morality, a universal human maxim, an ethical norm, but by my love for my actions.

Here we find a path whereby we can arrive at the insight that we harm the whole world and all beings in it if we do not rightly and properly unfold *our own* powers.

If you want to get the oven really hot, do not talk about your task in relation to the oven but instead supply it with fuel.

Our corporeal organism cannot provide the foundation for the cooperative action of will-endowed thought with thought-borne will.

Doing what we should, we furnish the arena where duty becomes action. An autonomous action is one whose intrinsic nature we allow to arise from us.

Living in love for our actions and *letting live* in understanding of another's will is the fundamental motto of the free human being.

We should not merely perceive development but also *live* it.

What we call *the good* is not what a person *ought* to do but what he *has the will* to do in unfolding his full, true human nature.

We must only carry out what accords with the standard we ourselves determine for our actions.

Without any need for compulsion, the free human being acts according to his own lights, *by commands that he gives himself.*

Our deeds are a part of universal occurrences, of the living fabric of the world.

4. A consciously knowing being cannot be unfree

Freedom is not *a given fact* of human existence but a *goal* of it.

The human soul can only *self-creatively engender* its insights within itself.

Soul life without insight or knowledge would be like a human organism without a head: in other words, nothing at all.

All true philosophers have been free artists working in concepts.

Only when we become aware that natural forces are nothing other than forms of the same spirit that also works within us will we see that we partake of freedom.

The essence of nature is that law and activity come asunder so that the latter appears to be governed by the former. The nature of freedom, by contrast, is that both join and cohere, so that the active principle manifests directly in the self-governing effect.

If thinking is to act in full freedom, it must also encompass the possibility of penetrating to a view of the world that derives the order of things from powers other than a personal God, and knows nothing of personal immortality and historical truths.

Whether some higher power or other governs our destiny for good or ill is not our concern. We ourselves must determine the path which we are to take.

Instead of bravely forging our way into the world we take fright at every difficulty and everywhere sense limits to our knowledge.

Our reason must once again become aware of itself as absolute, putting an end to its cowardly, slavish subordination to the oppressive power of facts.

Perceiving the idea within reality is true human communion.

Other than ourselves, we acknowledge no dominion in the world that directs and governs our actions.

An action is felt to be free in so far as it arises from the ideal part of my individual being. All other aspects of an action, irrespective of whether they arise from natural compulsions or the requirements of an ethical norm, are experienced as *unfree*.

Only when the objective essence of the thought world is realized so that a soul connection is perceived between ourselves and ethical motives as super-subjective experience can the nature of freedom be grasped.

Nature makes us into merely natural beings; society enables us to act lawfully. Only we ourselves can make *ourselves* into free beings.

Through our thinking we move from seeing ourselves as the *product* of reality to the *producer* of it.

No one at all has the right to dictate or determine the bounds of human cognition.

What human beings first heard as the voice of God outside them they now hear within them as autonomous power, and speak of this inner voice as identical with conscience.

Speaking metaphorically, our cognition is a continual delving into the ground of the world.

The free spirit acts according to his impulses — which are intuitions chosen by thinking from the totality of his world of ideas.

We have to confront and engage with the idea through our own experience, for otherwise we are subordinated and fall under its sway.

We are free to the extent that we can realize in our will the same mood of soul that lives in us when aware of the elaboration of purely ideal (spiritual) intuitions.

5. To err is to be human

In former times the *dogma of revelation* held sway. Today it is the *dogma of experience*.

Realists do not understand that the objective realm is idea, idealists that the ideal realm is objective.

The intrinsic nature of two diverging views or ways of thinking can often only be understood by regarding their divergence as the difference, for instance, between two images of the same tree which a camera takes from two different angles.

Anyone too cowardly to err cannot do battle for the truth.

If I say that the world is my idea, I have expressed the outcome of a process of thinking; and if my thinking is not applicable to the world, this outcome is an error.

While mere experience cannot reconcile opposites since it has reality but *not yet* idea, science or scholarship cannot achieve this reconciliation either because, though they do have the *idea*, they *no longer* have reality.

A truth that comes towards us from without always bears the stamp of uncertainty.

We have to have the courage to penetrate bravely into the realm of ideas, even at the risk of being mistaken.

Sensory illusion is not an error.

The basic mistake of many scientific endeavours today, especially, is the belief that these reflect experience, whereas in fact researchers are merely 'harvesting' the concepts they themselves have implanted in their enquiries.

A specialist training will sometimes broaden our horizons; often, though, it limits us in the same way that one might mistakenly travel from London to Paris via New York.

Someone who continually speaks of his 'divine self' is like someone who wishes to know nothing of tulips, violets, narcissi, roses, etc., but wishes to lump everything together under the concept of 'plant'.

We only fail to recognize what we ourselves have first rendered unrecognizable.

The divergence between two world outlooks does not mean that they do not both bring *true* reality to expression.

Anyone who gives himself up one-sidedly to thinking alone, to the development of our conceptual faculty, possesses scientific views that are empty and void of content. These possess a superfluous character precisely because they evade the realm into whose riddles they ought by rights to lead us. Someone who trusts only in the senses and seeks nothing but what *these* supply him succumbs to spiritual blindness: he gropes around the exterior of phenomena without finding the thread that would lead him into their inner reality, where apparent disorder reveals itself as lawfulness.

The continually prevailing tendency to acquire a world view that does not include thought, the idea, is highly characteristic of the dullness and cowardice of rationality today.

No opinion is so mistaken that one could not draw truth from it by really honest enquiry.

Anyone who has a sense for certain subtler laws at work in human logic and psychology knows that we often fail to discern the truth of a thought by allowing ourselves to be taken prisoner by the ideas surfacing prematurely in us that seemingly refute it.

Political agitators usually 'know' what is to be 'demanded' of others. They are far less aware of what they should demand of themselves.

An error that springs from the spirit is worth more than a truth growing in the soil of banality.

Nature researchers discover an external world that cannot be grasped by inner faculties; the mystic develops an inner life that grasps only emptiness as it seeks to take hold of an outer world it longs for.

As true as it is that everything of a sensory and material nature arises from spirit, so it is also true that all evils in the sense world arise from aberrations of the spirit.

Above all we must understand that every truth holds good only in its rightful place; that it remains true only for as long as it is asserted under the conditions that originally justified it.

6. Overcoming our sensory nature through the spirit is the goal of art and science

Every work of art requires its own aesthetic.

A piece of art is no less nature than a piece of nature; it is just that the natural lawfulness invested in it is in the form in which it appeared to the human spirit.

In a work of art everything depends on the extent to which the artist has implanted the idea in the material.

Two things are irreconcilable: active producing and contemplative consideration.

The whole exterior of an artist's work must give expression to its whole inner quality. In a natural product the latter remains hidden behind the former, and the enquiring human spirit first has to discern it.

In the same sense that one can say that *beauty* is unreal, untrue, is merely appearance since what it represents cannot be found anywhere in nature in such perfection, we can also say that beauty is truer than nature since it portrays what nature wishes to be but cannot attain.

Both cognitive and artistic activity depend on a person raising himself from reality as a product to being its producer, on progressing from the created world to creation, and from randomness to necessity.

A work of art is all the more important the more it possesses a quality that is not repeated anywhere and exists only in a single person.

A work of art of highest distinction is always original; for the spirit from which it arose is not found again anywhere in the world.

Beauty is not the divine in a garb of sensory reality. No, it is sensory reality in a divine garment.

Science hearkens to the lawfulness in nature; art does so equally, with the difference only that it also implants in the latter its raw material.

The artist does not bring the divine world to earth by letting it flow into the world but rather by raising the world to the divine sphere.

The infinite, which science seeks in the finite and tries to present in the idea, art imprints into a substance drawn from the existing world.

In a work of real art nothing must remain which the artist has not imprinted with *his own* spirit.

Sensory reality is transfigured in art so that it manifests as if it were spirit.

Mathematics is, in a sense, one vast poem.

The moment the senses cease their activity we find that a creative element infuses human activity.

Science looks *through* sensory reality to discover the idea, whereas art perceives the idea *within* sensory reality.

We cannot feel someone to be a really *strong* artist if he seems to the observer to be faithfully reproducing reality. He only is so when he compels us to accompany him as he furthers the world process creatively in his works.

In science, nature appears as the pure idea that encompasses every separate phenomenon. In art an external object appears as something that *portrays* this all-encompassing quality.

7. Nothing actually sunders itself from the rest of the world

The concept contains nothing that cannot also be found in the phenomenon; nor the phenomenon anything not also to be found in the concept.

What unfolds within us is not a repetition in thought of external reality but a real part of the world process.

To explain a thing and render it comprehensible means nothing other than to reincorporate it in the context which our own organization sundered it from.

The scientist perceives the totality of beings in the world such that the physical human being appears in his individual existence as a compendium, a unity, towards which all other natural processes and creatures point.

A thing I observe is no longer separate from me once I have perceived it.

The distinctive nature of every human being is something that must emerge from him and become a constituent of the process of evolution.

Cognition would be a vain and fruitless process if sensory experience were to present us with something perfect and complete.

All progress in science depends on becoming aware of the point where a particular phenomenon can be integrated into the harmony of the world of thought.

All concepts which reason creates — cause and effect, substance and inner attribute, body and soul, idea and reality, God and world, etc. — exist only to artificially separate the unity of reality. And, without erasing the content thus created, without mystically obscuring the clarity of rationality, reason must seek the inner unity within diversity.

Human beings contain ideal appearance while the world we perceive contains sensory appearance. Reality arises from the interworking of these two in cognition.

The whole ground of existence has resolved into the idea, has poured itself into it without restraint, so that we need seek it nowhere other than in the idea.

Through intuitions the human I, kindling in the soul, draws messages from above, from the world of spirit, in the same way that it draw messages from the physical world through feelings.

All life in the sensory world is oceanic flux in the spirit.

If our existence were connected with things in such a way that every occurrence in the world was, at the same time, *our* occurrence, then there would be no difference between us and other things.

In the spirit is naught but connection, while in nature is naught but separation. The spirit seeks the *genus*, while nature creates only individuals.

It is not the temporal existence of things but their inner nature that makes them perfect.

The meaning of separate realities, both intrinsically and for the rest of the world, only emerges when thinking draws connecting threads from one being to another.

What we discover in the observation of details is connected, link by link, through the coherent, unified world of our intuitions; and through thinking we incorporate into a whole again everything that we sundered through perception.

Yes: as ice is only one form in which water exists, so sensory things are only one form in which beings of soul and spirit exist.

The separate aspect of the world that I perceive as myself is infused with the stream of universal process.

By its very nature, the process of human cognition is a part of human evolution.

Our life is a continual fluctuation between experiencing universal world process and our individual existence.

We have arisen *from the world*; we are a 'small world' in which, in a sense, everything contained in the visible, and a large part of the invisible world, has been compressed.

It is not the task of enquiry and cognition to repeat in conceptual form something that is already present elsewhere but rather to create an entirely new domain which, together with the given world of the senses, gives rise to full reality.

What arises in the sensory world as feeling exists in the realm of spirit in just as all-permeating a way as air exists on earth.

We are not just leisurely observers of the world who repeat in our mind what occurs in the cosmos without our help, but rather are active co-creators of the world process; and cognition is the most perfect aspect of the organism of the universe.

We fulfil our highest spiritual needs when we incorporate into the objectively perceived world what this world reveals as its deepest secrets in our inner life.

8. The source of morality is spiritual pleasure in what we ourselves engender

A person who is free acts morally because he has a moral idea; but he does not act in order to create morality.

Our ethical ideals are our own free creation.

Nature's creativity is so great that the process of freely bringing forth all creatures out of the idea is one she repeats in every human individual by allowing moral actions to arise from the ideal ground of the individual.

In actions the thing of foremost importance is not by any means our feelings, whether selfish or selfless, but our right *judgement* about what is to be done.

Human moral action is a product of evolution.

A universally valid form of human ethics does not exist.

Like flowers, if they are to give us pleasure, the creations of the human spirit must fulfil these two requirements: they must be *genuine* and *fresh*.

We realize ourselves in our moral actions.

We do not act in the spirit of divine providence if we try to discover what it might command us to do, but instead by acting according to our own lights.

For someone who has developed harmoniously, so-called ideas of what is good do not lie *outside* but *within* his own being.

When we act morally, this is not to fulfil our duties and obligations but is, rather, the expression of our completely free nature.

Moral laws can only hold good as specific instances of natural laws.

9. We can only find nature outside us if we first know it within us

The same speech that reaches us from things is one we hear within ourselves.

Speaking of evolution in the realm of external nature only has inner justification if we also acknowledge this evolution in the realm of spirit and soul.

Only by making the *content of the world* into the *content of our thought* do we rediscover the context from which we have detached ourselves.

It would never occur to me to ask what the essential nature of things is if I did not discover within me something belonging to these things that I call this essence; and this is not something they give me of their own volition but rather something that I alone can draw from within me.

The same life that enlivens plants and animals as well as humankind, that endows crystals with their forms creates in us the ideals that give our existence purpose and meaning.

In the spirit all is continual *becoming.*

In coming to know nature we also come to know the I.

The world is not just familiar to us in appearance but appears—though only to thinking observation—as it is.

We do not learn to know ourselves by brooding upon our inner life but by grasping the true nature of stones, plants and animals around us; we *ourselves* are, you see, their being compressed into a single whole.

It is because our being is capable of love that nature becomes perceptible to us.

Just as the presence of a natural image is connected with our capacity for love, so our direct awareness of the human self is connected with our capacity for memory.

We gaze up to the starry heavens, and the delight that our soul experiences belongs to us. The eternal laws governing the stars, though, which we grasp in thought, in the *spirit*, do not belong to us but to the stars themselves.

Nature in her grandeur leads us to the divine; and our conscious search for the sources of truth traces the signs of her sleeping will.

Nature's encounter with itself unfolds in human consciousness.

While we seek to know nature with all the powers fitted for doing so, it is healthy to sense, simultaneously, that we are not thereby approaching true reality but distancing ourselves from it.

We dream up mathematical laws, and reality is kind enough to fulfil them for us.

In nature there lies something that a thousand facts will not reveal to us unless we possess the power of the perceiving spirit that reveals it to us as a single whole.

So you see, I really am the things of the world; or rather not I in so far as I am a perceiving subject, but inasmuch as I am part of the universal process of the world.

What good would it do me to discern the laws at work in the heavenly orbits of the stars without seeing how the powers which move the stars live in my soul at a higher level, and lead it to its goals?

Things speak to us, and our inner life speaks when we observe things.

As my self awakens, the things of the world undergo a spiritual *rebirth*.

World knowledge is born from self-knowledge.

A thinking that does not preclude itself from inner experience by prejudices of logic always ultimately comes to acknowledge the being holding sway within us who unites us with the whole world. This being enables us to overcome the opposition in us between inner and outer realities. In the stars and their changes and transformation, we can read the secrets of our soul.

We distance ourselves from reality by grasping it in a merely rational way.

We deny nature unless we become mystics.

But in *cognition* is accomplished something that

never occurs in the external world: world phenomena encounter and engage with their spiritual essence.

The inmost kernel of the world comes to life as spiritual content in self-knowledge.

Things can only appear to us in a way that accords with our nature.

If we experience the spirit within us, we do not need this spirit outside us in nature.

Only when we experience things within us do we find the key to the beauties of the outer world.

It is worth contemplating this thought: *the invisible will become visible*.

A wise person first learns to know the laws of the world; and then his wishes become powers that are realized.

We can come to the realization that observation of the visible world presents us with riddles that can never be resolved by the facts of this world.

If one person who has a rich inner life sees a

thousand things which signify nothing at all to someone poor in spirit, it becomes as clear as day that the *content* of reality is only the mirror image of the content of our spirit, and that all we receive from without is an empty form.

10. Outer freedom in social interaction depends upon the inner freedom of each individual

Whenever a person works for someone else, he has to find the foundation of his work in this other; and if someone is to work for the whole community then he must sense and feel the value, essence and meaning of this whole.

As long as you first enlarge your self to encompass the world self, then you can still act egoistically.

Each person increasingly comes to share in creating the edifice of society.

Modern consciousness is primarily characterized by the rejection of any and every norm.

Do not preach to people to be selfless but implant the keenest interests in them as a support to which their selfishness and egoism can cling.

The good of a totality of people working together is

all the greater the less each individual seeks the fruits of his own work, that is, the more he surrenders these fruits to his colleagues and the more his own needs are met not by his own work but by the work of others.

Thinkers have a decisive part to play in debates about the social question.

In so far as people regulate their *social interactions* in accordance with ordinary consciousness, powers intervene in these interactions that do not nurture wholesome human evolution.

The barometer of humanity's progressive evolution is in fact the view of freedom that people have, and the practical realization of this view.

Truth exists only where someone's personal interests, subjectivity and selfishness have been refined so that he is involved not only in his own person but in the whole world. Where people remain so small-minded that they only engage with the great concerns of the world by denying their personal, subjective interest, then they live in the worst, existential deception.

The laws of healthy human existence are

implanted in the archetypal foundation of the human soul as surely as primary mathematics are implanted there.

11. On occasion truth is destined to sound paradoxical in relation to contemporary realities

As strange as this sounds to modern ears: the brain is the most earthly product.

It is mistaken to claim that the brain is not the prerequisite for thinking that involves sensory perception. Another error is to deny that the spirit created the brain, and by means of it manifests in the physical world in thinking.

What an organ perceives also implicitly contains the power by means of which this organ itself develops.

Consciousness arises from powers that, in alliance with illusion, destroy life.

It lies in the very nature of the soul to *extinguish* something at first glance that belongs to the reality of the things perceived.

In everything we think about an external world of the senses we are involved with ideas that have been deadened.

In sensory life thoughts are mere shadows of how they manifest in the supersensible realm. And the will active in the world of the senses is, in comparison with its intrinsic nature in the supersensible realm, like a radiating power robbed of its light.

As strange as this sounds, our experience in the world of spirit shows us the following: the physical world is initially present for human beings as an outward context of facts; and we acquire knowledge of it when it has approached us in this form. By contrast, the world of spirit sends knowledge of itself in advance of its arrival, and the insight kindled in advance by it in the soul is the source of light that must shine upon the spiritual world so that it can reveal itself as reality.

The human soul is placed into the world in such a way that by its very nature it makes things different from how they are in reality.

We can only gain insight into the nature of birth and death if we regard them from the perspective of a realm outside the world of senses, where they do not exist.

The human body does not produce perceptions and soul experience in general but instead is a mirror for what occurs in the soul-spiritual realm beyond the body.

As well as our conscious mind containing truths, we also wish our convictions to be informed by the difficulties through which they were acquired.

As strange as this may sound for a superficial grasp of things, the following is true: though spiritual-scientific thoughts appear to float in cloud-cuckoo land, they give us the right perspective for leading our daily life.

The only true teachers of mysticism are those who have first been rigorous scientists and who therefore know how science is practised.

In the same way that the outward-oriented soul constructs machines, so the soul of our ancestors built up the human body itself.

12. With our I, you see, we are quite alone

Thinking is not an authentic indicator of the reality of the I.

The I that understands itself can rely on nothing other than itself.

The I, as our true, intrinsic being, remains entirely invisible.

We would not be human beings if we were not closed off as I from everything else. But nor would we be human in the truest sense if, as self-contained I, we did not enlarge ourselves again to encompass the universal I.

We should always keep in mind that we are in fact being egotistic if we love an opinion because we ourselves hold it.

Body and soul surrender to the I in order to serve it; but the I surrenders itself to the spirit so that the latter may fulfil it.

Thus while our surroundings between birth and death speak to us through the organs of our bodies, after we have laid aside all these bodies the language of our new surroundings speaks directly within the 'inmost sanctum' of the I.

The spirit forms the I from within outwards, and the mineral world from outside inwards.

Everything the I within the world of senses desires of the spiritual realm it possesses when the senses are no longer there.

What many people say to me I do not attend to, for I can usually also tell myself the same thing. But what I yearn for is what only very few can tell me.

If you reflect on the nature of biography, of a human life, you will see that in a spiritual sense *every human being is a distinct and separate species.*

Is anyone able to prove he exists by deduction?

As the centre of the physical body is in the brain, so the centre of the soul is in the I.

Truth is no rigid, dead
system of concepts
capable only of assuming a single form;
it is a living ocean
in which the human spirit lives
on whose surface waves of the most varied form
can arise and appear.

Bibliography

Numbers below refer to the GA (Gesamtausgabe or complete edition) of Steiner's works in German. English titles are given where these are available

1 *Einleitungen zu Goethes Naturwissenschaftliche Schriften* [*Goethean Science*, Mercury Press, 1988]

2 *Grundlinien einer Erkenntnistheorie der Goetheschen Weltanschauung, mit besonderer Rücksicht auf Schiller* [*Goethe's Theory of Knowledge: An Outline of the Epistemology of His Worldview*, SteinerBooks, 2008]

3 *Wahrheit und Wissenschaft. Vorspiel einer 'Philosophie der Freiheit'* [*Truth and Knowledge: Introduction to The Philosophy of Spiritual Activity*, SteinerBooks, 1981]

4 *Die Philosophie der Freiheit. Grundzüge einer modernen Weltanschauung – Seelische Beobachtungsresultate nach naturwissenschaftlicher Methode* [*The Philosophy of Freedom: The Basis for a Modern World Conception*, Rudolf Steiner Press, 2011]

6 *Goethes Weltanschauung* [*Goethe's World View*, Mercury Press, 1985]

7 *Die Mystik im Aufgange des neuzeitlichen Geisteslebens und ihr Verhältnis zur modernen Weltanschauung* [*Mystics After Modernism*, Anthroposophic Press, 2000]

posophie und Berichte aus den Zeitschriften 'Lucifer' und 'Lucifer-Gnosis' 1903–1908

35 *Philosophie und Anthroposophie. Gesammelte Aufsätze 1904–1923*

94 *Kosmogonie. Populärer Okkultismus. Das Johannes-Evangelium. Die Theosophie an Hand des Johannes-Evangeliums* [*An Esoteric Cosmology,* St. George Publications 1978]

GA Page References for Each Quoted Passage

The way a person thinks...	GA 34, p. 451
Thought has proven itself...	GA 18, p. 621
Thinking may play a secondary role...	GA 4, p. 39
One may carry all the world's knowledge...	GA 30, p. 423
Thinking has to strengthen itself to act...	GA 35, p. 423
The distinctive nature of thinking...	GA 4, p. 42
Ordinary thinking gives pictures...	GA 35, p. 289
I can never observe my thinking...	GA 4, p. 43
The whole human body is formed...	GA 9, p. 33
Unprejudiced observation shows...	GA 4, p. 56
However, there are people...	GA 2, p. 143
I should never say...	GA 4, p. 60
All thinking leads only to the point...	GA 32, p. 330
It is on this that our dual nature is based...	GA 4, p. 60f.
Someone who relies on his thinking...	GA 30, p. 105f.
Our thinking is the interpreter...	GA 2, p. 66
Having driven thinking into inner...	GA 35, pp. 289f.
In thinking we have the element...	GA 4, p. 91
The human body is formed...	GA 9, p. 34
In sensing and feeling...	GA 4, p. 91
The act of cognition...	GA 4, p. 92
Thinking is a human organ...	GA 2, p. 63
In ordinary consciousness...	GA 20, p. 161
The full reality of a thing arises...	GA 4, p. 107
We can only grasp the nature of thinking...	GA 4, p. 146
The reality active in thinking...	GA 4, p. 147

Manifold consciousnesses think...	GA 1, p. 164
However confused my thinking...	GA 9, p. 183
If we have the capacity for this...	GA 1, p. 177
What the spirit finds as unity...	GA 2, p. 121
What can least be learned...	GA 31, p. 158
For human beings to be...	GA 2, p. 125
The world's cultural content...	GA 32, pp. 307f.
The active principle in all other things...	GA 6, p. 92
A true individual will be the one...	GA 4, p. 110
In grasping truth the soul unites...	GA 9, p. 45
The human spirit never, in truth...	GA 4, p. 251
Only when the world of ideas...	GA 6, p. 28

3. We do not act because we should...

	GA 2, p. 126
Will without idea would be nothing...	GA 1, p. 198
The motive for action does not lie...	GA 2, p. 125
To illumine the laws of our actions...	GA 7, p. 36
The heart follows the head...	GA 31, p. 167
If all natural processes are only...	GA 1, p. 199
To perform an action for its own sake...	GA 1, p. 203
The same power that rescues us...	GA 35, p. 419
We only act in real freedom...	GA 1, p. 203
And even if different people...	GA 31, p. 138
The human being is his own lawgiver...	GA 2, p. 125
Our usual thinking capacity...	GA 35, p. 281
The path to the heart passes...	GA 4, p. 25